Mapping the Continents

Mapping Australia and Oceania, and Antarctica

Paul Rockett

with artwork by Mark Ruffle

Crabtree Publishing Company

www.crabtreebooks.com

Crabtree Publishing Company
www.crabtreebooks.com
1-800-387-7650

Published in Canada
616 Welland Ave.
St. Catharines, ON
L2M 5V6

Published in the United States
PMB 59051, 350 Fifth Ave.
59th Floor,
New York, NY

Published in 2017 by CRABTREE PUBLISHING COMPANY.

First published in 2015 by The Watts Publishing Group
(An imprint of Hachette Children's Group)
Copyright © The Watts Publishing Group 2015

Author: Paul Rockett

Editorial director: Kathy Middleton

Editors: Adrian Cole, and Ellen Rodger

Proofreader: Wendy Scavuzzo

Series design and illustration:
  Mark Ruffle, www.rufflebrothers.com

Prepress technician: Katherine Berti

Print and production coordinator: Katherine Berti

Printed in Canada/072016/PB20160525

Picture credits:
Jon Arnold Images/Alamy: 27b; EPA/Ettore Ferrari/Alamy: 23; Jinny Goodman/Alamy: 19b; Nick Haslam/Alamy: 25t; G Brad Lewis/Science Faction/Corbis: 15t; Julie McNeil/CC Wikimedia: 9c; Johan Mollerberg/Dreamstime: 24t; NASA/Johnson Space Center: 14b; NOAA: 29b; Chris Rainier/Corbis: 19c; Percy Smith/CC Wikimedia: 8c; George Steinmetz/Corbis: 21t; Jim Sugar/Corbis: 17t; Stephen Tappley/Dreamstime: 17b; Travelling-Light/Dreamstime: 18b; Travelscape Images/Alamy: 24c; CC Wikimedia: 06-07, 9c, 22.

Library and Archives Canada Cataloguing in Publication

Rockett, Paul, author
    Mapping Australia and Oceania, and Antarctica / Paul Rockett.

(Mapping the continents)
Includes index.
Issued in print and electronic formats.
ISBN 978-0-7787-2614-2 (hardback).--
ISBN 978-0-7787-2620-3 (paperback).--
ISBN 978-1-4271-1781-6 (html)

        1. Australia--Juvenile literature. 2. Oceania--Juvenile literature.
3. Antarctica--Juvenile literature. 4. Cartography--Australia--Juvenile
literature. 5. Cartography--Oceania--Juvenile literature. 6. Cartography--
Antarctica--Juvenile literature. 7. Australia--Geography--Juvenile literature.
8. Oceania--Geography--Juvenile literature. 9. Antarctica--Geography--
Juvenile literature.
I. Title.

DU17.R64 2016   j914   C2016-902654-X
                                     C2016-902655-8

Library of Congress Cataloging-in-Publication Data

Names: Rockett, Paul, author.
Title: Mapping Australia and Oceania, and Antarctica / Paul Rockett.
Description: New York, New York : Crabtree Publishing Co., 2017. |
Series: Mapping the continents | Includes index. |
Identifiers: LCCN 2016016674 (print) | LCCN 2016024421 (ebook) |
ISBN 9780778726142 (reinforced library binding) |
ISBN 9780778726203 (pbk.) |
ISBN 9781427117816 (electronic HTML)
Subjects: LCSH: Australia--Juvenile literature. | Oceania--Juvenile
  literature. | Antarctica--Juvenile literature. |
  Cartography--Australia--Juvenile literature. |
  Cartography--Oceania--Juvenile literature. |
  Cartography--Antarctica--Juvenile literature. |
  Geography--Australia--Juvenile literature. | Geography--Oceania--Juvenile
  literature. | Geography--Antarctica--Juvenile literature. |
  Australia--Description and travel--Juvenile literature. |
  Oceania--Description and travel--Juvenile literature. |
  Antarctica--Description and travel--Juvenile literature.
Classification: LCC DU96 .R64 2017 (print) | LCC DU96 (ebook) |
DDC 919.5--dc23
LC record available at https://lccn.loc.gov/2016016674

Contents

Where is Australia/Oceania?

Out of the seven continents of the world, Australia/Oceania is the smallest. It is made up of the islands of Australia, Tasmania, and New Zealand, as well as Papua New Guinea, and thousands of small islands in the Pacific Ocean.

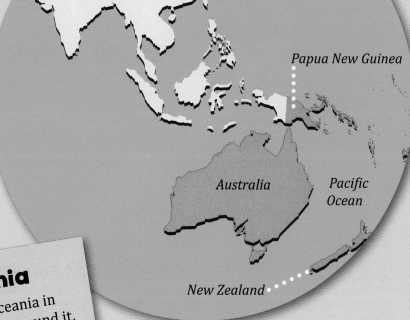

Papua New Guinea

Australia

Pacific Ocean

New Zealand

Locating Australia/Oceania

We can describe the position of Australia/Oceania in relation to the areas of land and water that surround it, as well as by using the points on a compass.

Australia/Oceania is between the Indian Ocean and the Pacific Ocean

Australia/Oceania is north of Antarctica

Antarctica

A collection of continents

Some geographers believe there is more than one continent within the area of Australia/Oceania.

Australia

They define a continent as being made up of a single landmass and therefore view Australia as a continent.

Zealandia

Others see New Zealand as part of a separate continent called Zealandia. This includes an area of land surrounding New Zealand that is under the sea.

Land area under water ••••••••

Australasia

Some geographers believe that all of the islands within the central and South Pacific are part of a continent called Oceania. Australia is sometimes included in this group.

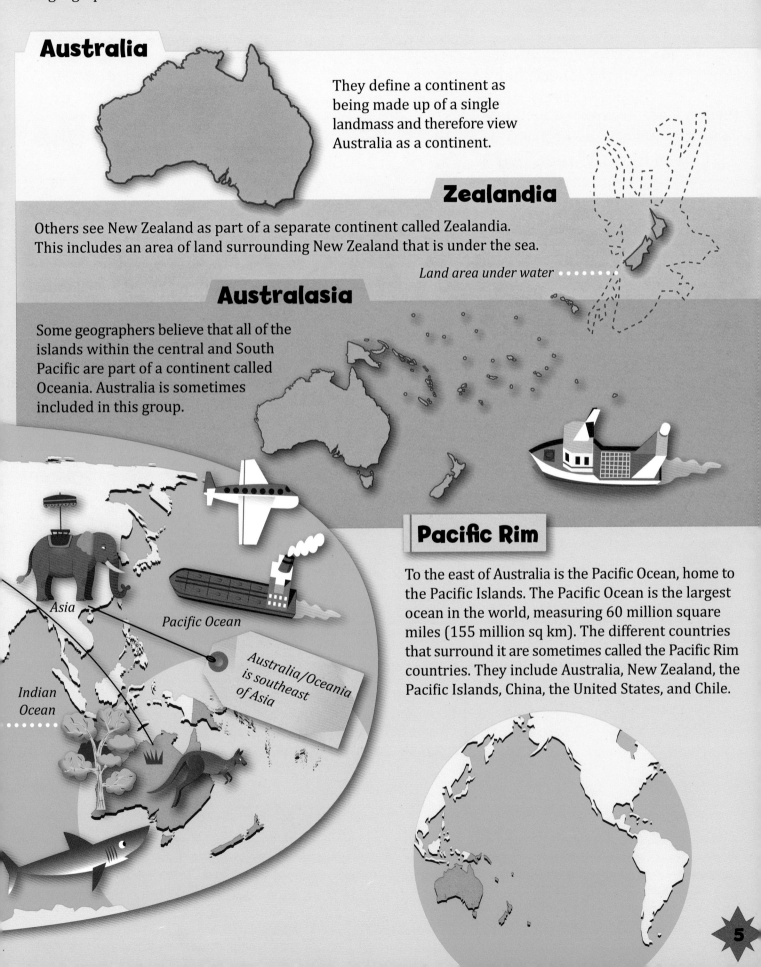

Asia

Pacific Ocean

Indian Ocean

Australia/Oceania is southeast of Asia

Pacific Rim

To the east of Australia is the Pacific Ocean, home to the Pacific Islands. The Pacific Ocean is the largest ocean in the world, measuring 60 million square miles (155 million sq km). The different countries that surround it are sometimes called the Pacific Rim countries. They include Australia, New Zealand, the Pacific Islands, China, the United States, and Chile.

Countries

There are 14 countries in the continent of Australia/Oceania, and thousands of small islands. Many of these islands are not independent countries, but are the overseas territory of countries from around the world. These countries are called **sovereign states** and have an important influence on how the islands are governed.

Northern Mariana Islands
*(**sovereign state**: United States)*

Palau

Federated States of Micronesia

Papua New Guinea

Australia

Solomon Islands

New Caledonia
*(**sovereign state**: France)*

NT

Qld

WA

SA

NSW

Vic.

Tas.

Te Ika-a-Māui (North Island)

Te Waipounamu (South Island)

New Zealand

Australian states

Australia is divided up into seven main states:
NSW = New South Wales
NT = Northern Territory
Qld = Queensland
SA = South Australia
Tas. = Tasmania
Vic. = Victoria
WA = Western Australia

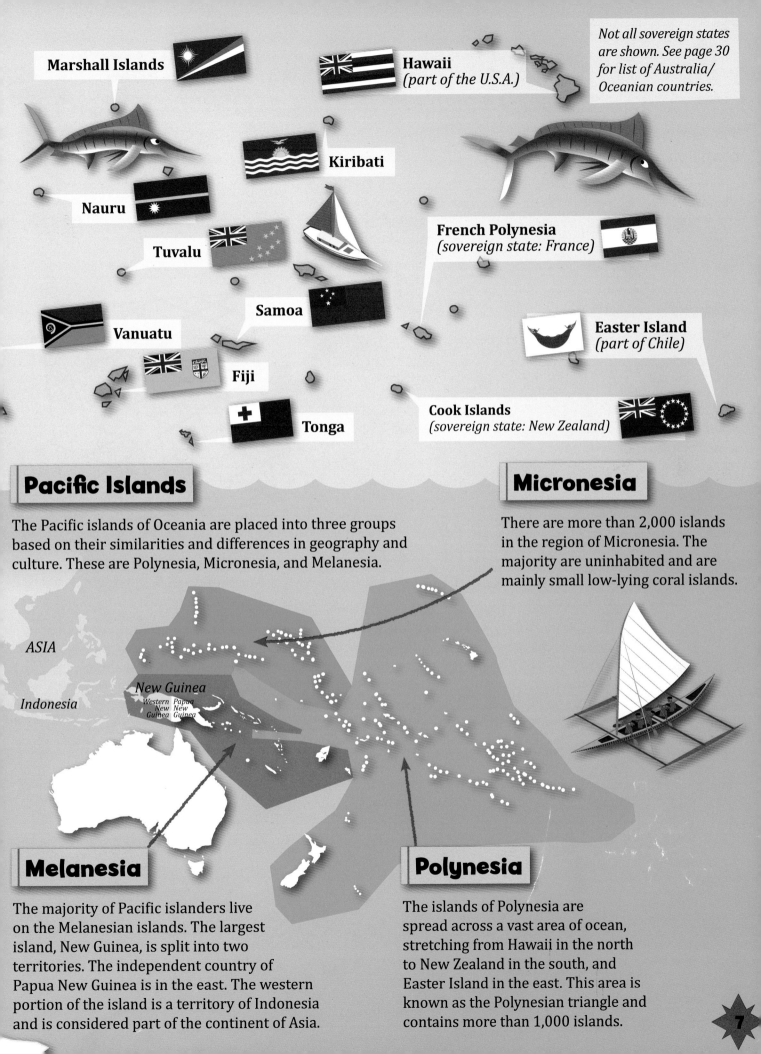

Marshall Islands

Hawaii
(part of the U.S.A.)

Not all sovereign states are shown. See page 30 for list of Australia/ Oceanian countries.

Kiribati

Nauru

French Polynesia
(sovereign state: France)

Tuvalu

Vanuatu

Samoa

Easter Island
(part of Chile)

Fiji

Tonga

Cook Islands
(sovereign state: New Zealand)

Pacific Islands

The Pacific islands of Oceania are placed into three groups based on their similarities and differences in geography and culture. These are Polynesia, Micronesia, and Melanesia.

Micronesia

There are more than 2,000 islands in the region of Micronesia. The majority are uninhabited and are mainly small low-lying coral islands.

ASIA

Indonesia

New Guinea
Western New Guinea *Papua New Guinea*

Melanesia

The majority of Pacific islanders live on the Melanesian islands. The largest island, New Guinea, is split into two territories. The independent country of Papua New Guinea is in the east. The western portion of the island is a territory of Indonesia and is considered part of the continent of Asia.

Polynesia

The islands of Polynesia are spread across a vast area of ocean, stretching from Hawaii in the north to New Zealand in the south, and Easter Island in the east. This area is known as the Polynesian triangle and contains more than 1,000 islands.

Early maps and ownership

The original inhabitants of Australia/Oceania are thought to have traveled down from different parts of Asia up to 60,000 years ago.

The descendants of those settlers are described as **Indigenous** peoples. In Australia they are the Aborigines, and in New Zealand they are the Maoris. There is also a smaller group, known as the Torres Strait Islanders, in the north of Queensland, Australia, and in the Melanesian Islands south of Papua New Guinea.

Ocean maps

Early inhabitants of the Marshall Islands, in Micronesia, used stick charts to help **navigate** around the Pacific Ocean. Made from strips of coconut fibre and shells, these charts mapped parts of the ocean, marking out islands, waves, and **ocean currents**.

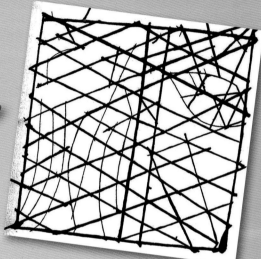

Islanders memorized the stick charts before setting out to sea in their canoes.

Aboriginal mapping

Australian Aborigines drew maps with symbols that marked the location of water holes and other landscape features. The maps were usually drawn on the ground, and often included stories that describe the creation of the world, called the Dreamtime. Here are some Aboriginal symbols:

Cliff or sandhill

Water

Water holes connected by running water

Star

Sitting-down place

8

The European invasion

European explorers arrived in the 1500s. Over the next 300 years, Europe took control of Australia/Oceania. Many of the people who live here now are descended from Europeans.

1519–1521
Portuguese navigator Ferdinand Magellan sails across the Pacific Ocean, reaching Guam.

1606
Dutch explorer Willem Janszoon is the first European to land on northern Australia.

This map from 1644 is drawn from the accounts given by explorers such as Abel Tasman. Much of the Australian coast was still to be explored, and the north is shown connected to the island of New Guinea.

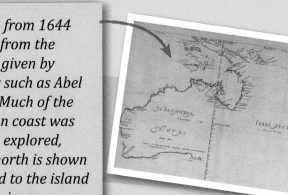

1642–1645
Dutchman Abel Tasman sails around parts of Australia and visits New Zealand, New Guinea, Tonga, and Fiji. He names Australia "New Holland."

1768
English explorer Captain James Cook begins a voyage around the Pacific. He lands at Botany Bay, Australia, in 1770. Cook made three voyages exploring Australia/Oceania.

1788
The British claim control of the eastern side of Australia, calling it New South Wales. They send a boat of **convicts** off to Australia to be housed in Port Jackson (Sydney).

1840
In New Zealand, Maori chiefs sign the Treaty of Waitangi— an agreement between the British government and Maori tribes.

1907
New Zealand is granted independence from Britain.

1901
Australia becomes independent from British rule.

1860s–1872
Series of battles between British settlers and the Maori over land and **colonial** control.

Colonial control

The Pacific islands have been controlled by the Dutch, Spanish, British, French, German, Japanese, and United States governments. The islands eventually began to gain independence, starting with Samoa in 1962 to Palau in 1994.

Climate

Australia/Oceania enjoys a warm **climate**, with bright sunshine and cool breezes by the coast. However, the weather in this continent creates dry deserts and humid rainforests, and can also trigger destructive fires, storms, and devastating droughts.

Climate zones

Australia/Oceania has four climate zones. Each zone experiences different weather conditions that shape the plants and animals and the lifestyles of those who live there.

tropical humid
dry
Mediterranean
marine west coast

Hawaii: 88–69 °F (31.1–20.6 °C)

French Polynesia: 82–70 °F (28–21 °C)

Cook Islands: 77–66 °F (25–19 °C)

Easter Island: 70–59 °F (21–15 °C)

Papua New Guinea: 88–72 °F (31–22 °C)

Fiji: 83–69 °F (28.5–18.3 °C)

Auckland, New Zealand: 59–48.2 °F (15–9 °C)

Queenstown, New Zealand: 50–34 °F (10–1 °C)

Darwin, Australia: 86–67 °F (30.5–19.3 °C)

Alice Springs, Australia: 67–39°F (19.7–4.1°C)

Canberra, Australia: 53–32°F (11.4–0.1°C)

Perth, Australia: 64–46°F (17.9–8°C)

Coldest month

The map shows the minimum and maximum temperatures during the coldest month of July.

Even in the coldest months, from June to August, the temperatures in Australia/Oceania are warmer than some European countries in the summer months.

Climate catastrophes

Bushfires

Australia has a largely hot and dry climate. During the hottest months of the year—December to February—it often experiences heat waves and droughts. This causes the forests and grasslands to become extremely dry. The dry vegetation can catch fire easily and the fire spreads quickly. These are known as bushfires.

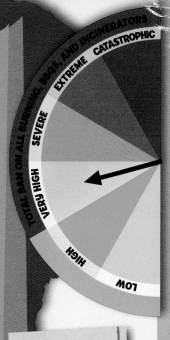

This is a fire danger chart used to warn of bushfires. The ratings are based on temperature, humidity, wind speed, and dryness of the vegetation.

El Niño

The climate of the Pacific islands is influenced by changing wind pressures and temperatures that cross over the Pacific Ocean. Sometimes extreme weather conditions occur, such as an El Niño, causing dramatic changes to a country's climate.

Normal year

Normally, strong winds blow warm surface water west across the Pacific Ocean, toward Australia/Oceania. This increases rainfall and encourages tropical rain forest conditions.

Key:
warm water
cold water
wind

Pacific Ocean

Australia

South America

El Niño year

An El Niño occurs when the westward wind changes direction and the warm surface water is blown east, toward the coast of South America.

Warm water moving toward South America brings heavy storms and a rise in **sea level**, which can cause flooding. Without warm water, which turns to rain, areas of Australia/Oceania can be affected by **drought**.

Australia

Pacific Ocean

South America

Wildlife

The vast open landscape in Australia and the dense island forests in the Pacific are home to some of the world's oddest and most dangerous wildlife.

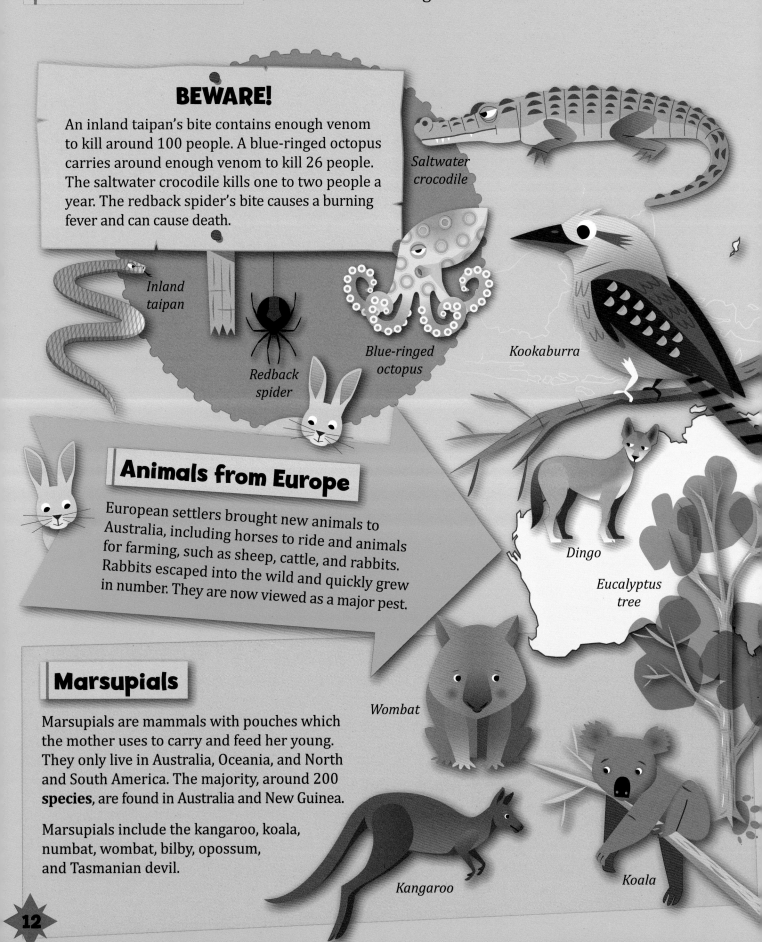

BEWARE!

An inland taipan's bite contains enough venom to kill around 100 people. A blue-ringed octopus carries around enough venom to kill 26 people. The saltwater crocodile kills one to two people a year. The redback spider's bite causes a burning fever and can cause death.

Saltwater crocodile

Inland taipan

Redback spider

Blue-ringed octopus

Kookaburra

Dingo

Eucalyptus tree

Animals from Europe

European settlers brought new animals to Australia, including horses to ride and animals for farming, such as sheep, cattle, and rabbits. Rabbits escaped into the wild and quickly grew in number. They are now viewed as a major pest.

Marsupials

Marsupials are mammals with pouches which the mother uses to carry and feed her young. They only live in Australia, Oceania, and North and South America. The majority, around 200 **species**, are found in Australia and New Guinea.

Marsupials include the kangaroo, koala, numbat, wombat, bilby, opossum, and Tasmanian devil.

Wombat

Koala

Kangaroo

Monotremes

Monotremes are mammals that lay eggs. They are only found in Australia and New Guinea. There are two kinds of monotremes in the world: the echidna and the platypus. Both look like a strange combination of different creatures: the platypus has a duck-like bill and beaver-like tail, whereas the echidna has long hedgehog-like spines on its back and a long snout like an anteater.

Platypus

Echidna

Flatback sea turtle

Great white shark

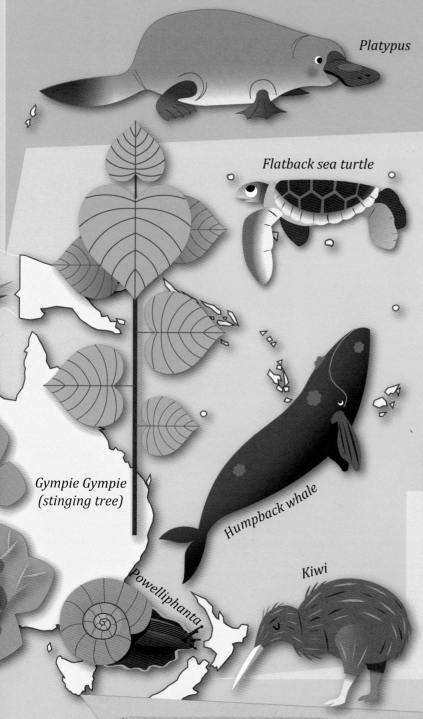

Pandanus tree

Gympie Gympie (stinging tree)

Humpback whale

Powelliphanta

Kiwi

Flightless birds

There are more flightless birds in New Zealand than anywhere else in the world. They include kiwis, takahē, kakapo, and penguins.

Emus are large flightless birds that live in Australia.

Tasmanian devil

The Tasmanian devil is only the size of a small dog, but is the largest carnivorous marsupial. Its name comes from the fact that it only lives on Tasmania and makes piercing shrieks and screams.

Emu

Natural landmarks

Australia/Oceania is still largely uninhabited. Huge deserts, steamy rain forests, coral reefs, fiery volcanoes, and high mountains can all be found on the continent.

Great Barrier Reef

The Great Barrier Reef is the largest living structure on Earth. It's made up of billions of corals, stretching more than 1,243 miles (2,000 km) in length. It's one of the richest ecosystems on Earth, home to thousands of different species of marine life, including mollusks, parrotfish, and sharks.

Uluru

Near the center of Australia is the iconic giant sandstone **monolith**, Uluru. It's 1,142 feet (348 m) high, and changes color in the sunlight, glowing red at dawn and sunset.

It's a landmark that is sacred to the local Aboriginal peoples, as it is the focus of many of their creation stories.

Atolls

The Pacific Ocean is home to the largest number of **atolls** in the world. These are flat coral islands that encircle a shallow body of water, known as a lagoon. They form around the remains of sunken islands that were created by the buildup of lava from underwater volcanoes.

Pinnacles Desert

Great Barrier Reef

Great Dividing Range

Coral Sea Islands

Uluru

Darling River

Murray River

Blue Mountains

Wave Rock

Atafu is an atoll that is part of the islands of Tokelau.

Hawaii

The island of Hawaii is made up of five volcanoes. These include one of the largest active volcanoes in the world, Mauna Loa, measuring 13,677 feet (4,169 m) in height. It also has the world's tallest mountain, the dormant volcano Mauna Kea. It measures 33,474 feet (10,203 m) up from the seabed, although only 13,796 feet (4,205 m) of this is above sea level.

Hawaii

Kauai

Oahu

Maui

Mauna Kea

Kohala

Hualalai

Mauna Loa

Kilauea

Marshall Islands

Kiribati Islands

The volcanic activity on Hawaii is causing the island to grow in size. Lava from the Kilauea volcano flows into the Pacific Ocean and cools to form new land.

Nauru

Banabu

Caroline Island

Tuvalu

Tokelau

Makatea

Tuamotu

- ◉ High island rock
- ◖ Atoll coral reef

Niue

Henderson

Ring of Fire

New Zealand's Southern Alps is a mountain range which has formed where the Pacific and Indo-Australian **tectonic plates** meet. It is also the beginning of the Ring of Fire—a string of 452 volcanoes that are located around the edge of the Pacific Ocean and form a rough horseshoe shape.

The Ring of Fire volcanoes are some of the most active volcanoes in the world. There, the edge of the Pacific Plate expands and collides with **neighboring** tectonic plates, causing volcanic activity and earthquakes.

Mount Taranaki

Rotorua **thermal geysers**

Southern Alps

Aoraki

Ring of Fire

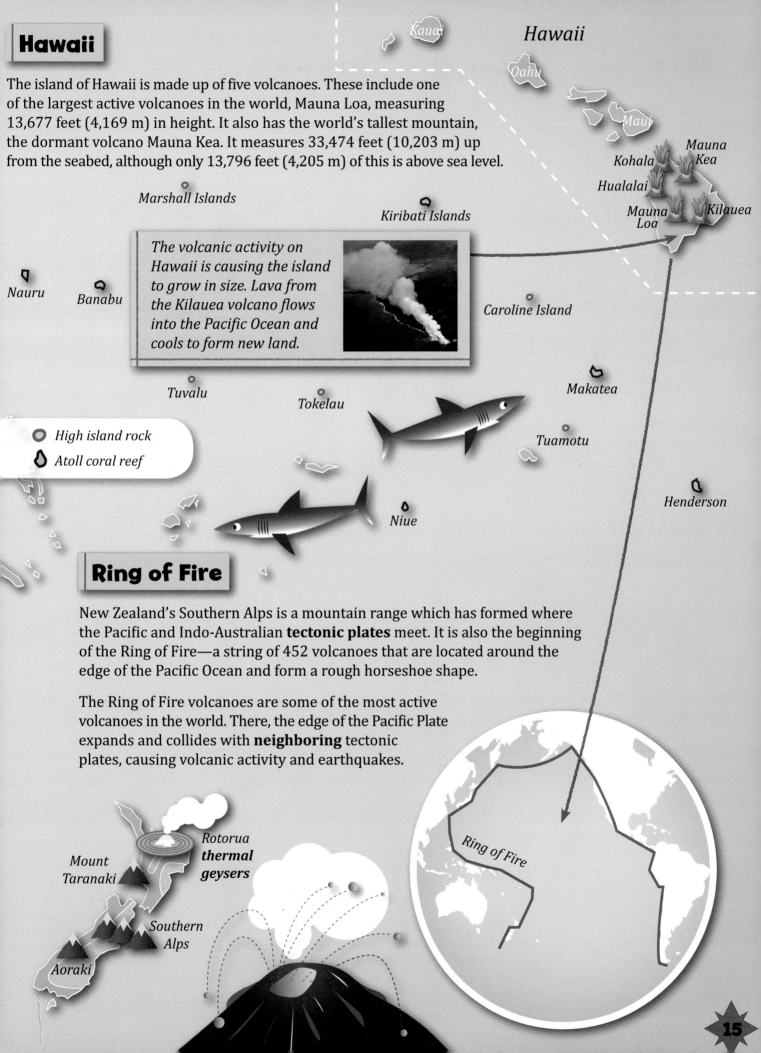

Human-made landmarks

The human-made landmarks in Australia/Oceania show off the amazing building skills of people in the past and today.

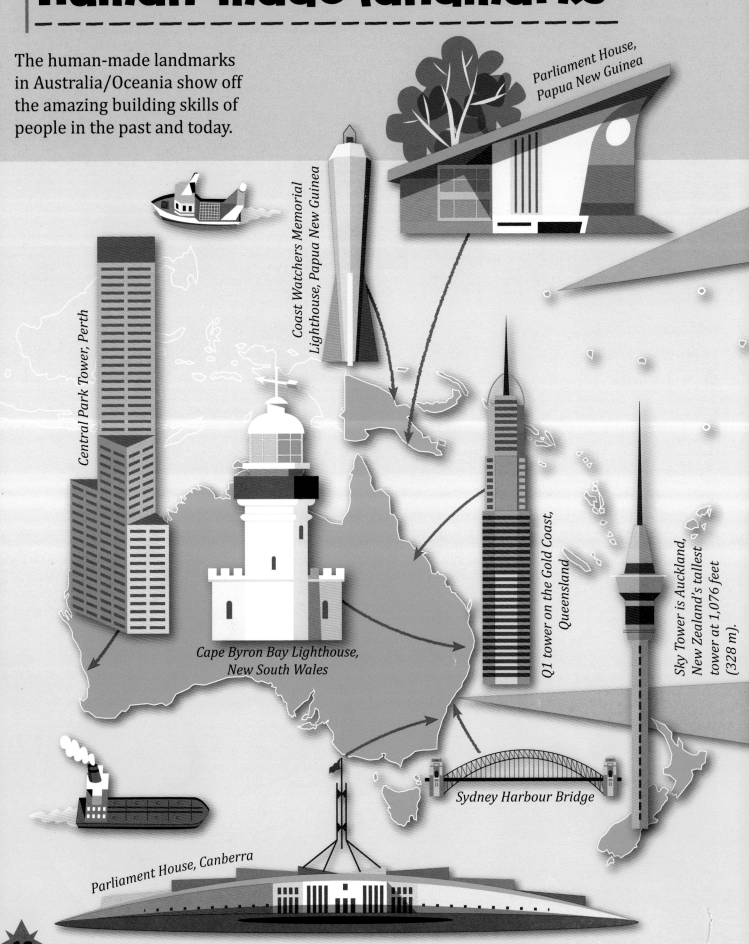

Parliament House, Papua New Guinea

Coast Watchers Memorial Lighthouse, Papua New Guinea

Central Park Tower, Perth

Cape Byron Bay Lighthouse, New South Wales

Q1 tower on the Gold Coast, Queensland

Sky Tower is Auckland, New Zealand's tallest tower at 1,076 feet (328 m).

Sydney Harbour Bridge

Parliament House, Canberra

Nan Madol

Nan Madol (below) is an ancient ruined city that lies off the east coast of the island of Pohnpei, part of the Federated States of Micronesia. Between 500 B.C.E. and 1500 C.E., people there constructed royal palaces, tombs, and other buildings, using heavy stone and coral. No one is sure how the stones got there. According to local legend, they were flown in by black magic!

Nan Madol was the center of a ruling empire that had disappeared by the time the Europeans arrived.

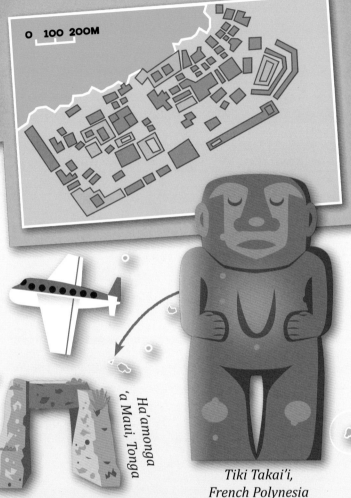

O 100 200M

Ha'amonga 'a Maui, Tonga

Tiki Takai'i, French Polynesia

Moai

Easter Island is famous for its giant statues that stare blankly across its landscape. They are called moai and were carved by the Rapa Nui people who lived on the island. They were made from around 1000 C.E. until the late 1600s.

It's thought that the moai were created to represent powerful chiefs, keeping watch over their people.

= Moai

Easter Island

Sydney Opera House

The most famous building in Australia is the Sydney Opera House. It was designed by Danish architect, Jørn Utzon. Concerts, plays, and ballets are performed here, as well as operas.

The sails of great ships inspired the design of the [sail]-like roofs. The design connects the buildings to its location beside Sydney Harbor.

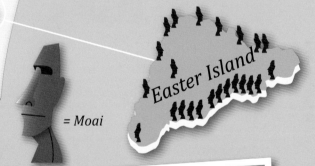

The majority of the Easter Island figures are carved from hardened volcanic ash, and all but seven face inland.

Settlements

Most of Australia/Oceania's settlements have been built along the coastline. It's cooler there than it is inland, and it's also the place where settlers would have first arrived, building their camps and colonies near to where their canoes and ships docked.

Indigenous land

In 1995, the Indigenous Land Corporation was set up in Australia. It helps Aboriginal communities regain control of and manage their land. This land is kept clear of cattle farming and mining industries. There, Aboriginal peoples can live within natural environments, practicing the traditions of their ancestors.

Perth

Adelaide

■ Major cities

■ Inner regional Australia

■ Outer regional Australia

□ Very remote Australia

■ Areas of Indigenous land

Perth

Perth is the largest city in Western Australia and one of the most isolated cities in the world. The next closest big city, Adelaide, is 1,307 miles (2,104 km) away.

Huli tribe

The Huli people live in the Tari rain forest in the Southern Highlands of Papua New Guinea. Their way of life has changed little since they first had contact with Europeans in 1935.

Huli men and women live in separate huts. The men are hunter-gatherers and the women are farmers, growing vegetables such as sweet potatoes and yams. The women also share their homes with pigs, which are used as a form of currency.

The Huli people still wear traditional clothing for special occasions. They paint their faces and the men wear wigs made from their own hair, decorated with feathers from tropical birds.

Christchurch

New Zealand experiences thousands of small earthquakes each year. Most are minor, causing small **tremors**. However, when big earthquakes strike they can cause terrible damage to homes and cities.

A major earthquake hit New Zealand's second-largest city, Christchurch, in 2011. The force was greater than anything the city had previously experienced; it destroyed around 60 percent of the city center and killed 185 people. It took two years to make the center safe, and reopen buildings to the public.

City center

Tremors likely to be felt

Possible contents damage

Possible structural damage to buildings

Christchurch Cathedral was damaged by the 2011 earthquake.

Industries

Farms, big and small, are essential for food and trade within the islands of Australia/ Oceania. The islands' isolation and natural beauty make them popular with tourists, and many local people have jobs connected to tourism. Mining and manufacturing are also big business for the larger islands.

Imports and exports

Australia/Oceania's nearest continental neighbor is Asia. The short distance between them means goods do not have very far to travel.

The blue arrows around the Pacific Ocean show the route a freight ship from Asia takes as it delivers and picks up goods from ports around Australia.

ASIA

Imports
*The main goods Australia/ Oceania **imports** from Asia include computers, televisions, toys, games, sporting goods, and furniture.*

Lihir, Papua New Guinea

—— *railway*

Indian Pacific railway

Ooldea

Loongana

Exports
*The main **exports** from Australia are iron, coal, gold, and professional services.*

Transportation connections

To help reach many of the distant places in Australia, there are more than 400 airports dotted around the country. There are also major rail networks that transport people and goods across its landscape.

The Indian Pacific railway includes the world's longest stretch of dead-straight railway track. The line travels straight for 297 miles (478 km) between Loongana and Ooldea.

Main industries in Australia/Oceania

Crops:
- 🍎 Fruit
- 🌽 Corn
- Oats
- Rice
- 🍬 Sugar
- 🍇 Vineyards
- 🌾 Wheat

Industries:
- Mining
- 🐟 Fishing
- 🚗 Automobiles
- High tech
- 💼 Tourism

Livestock:
- 🐄 Cattle
- 🐑 Sheep

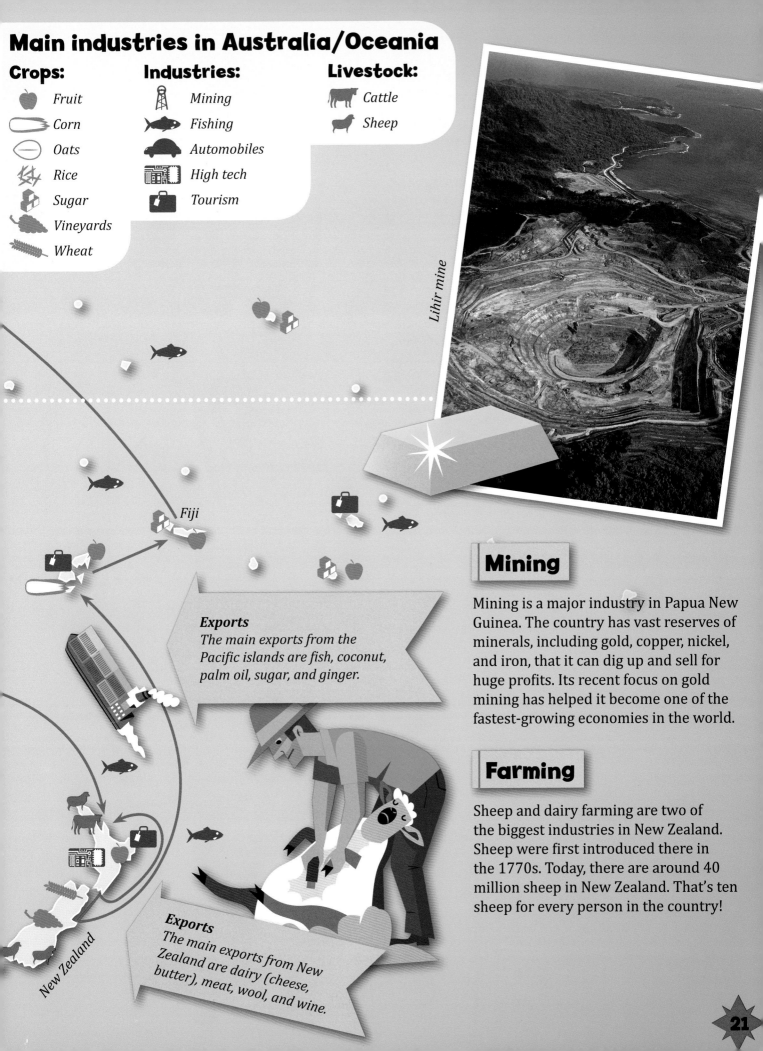

Lihir mine

Fiji

New Zealand

Exports
The main exports from the Pacific islands are fish, coconut, palm oil, sugar, and ginger.

Exports
The main exports from New Zealand are dairy (cheese, butter), meat, wool, and wine.

Mining

Mining is a major industry in Papua New Guinea. The country has vast reserves of minerals, including gold, copper, nickel, and iron, that it can dig up and sell for huge profits. Its recent focus on gold mining has helped it become one of the fastest-growing economies in the world.

Farming

Sheep and dairy farming are two of the biggest industries in New Zealand. Sheep were first introduced there in the 1770s. Today, there are around 40 million sheep in New Zealand. That's ten sheep for every person in the country!

Sports

Australia/Oceania takes part in many international sporting events, producing top-ranking rugby players, swimmers, and tennis stars. It's also home to their own sports, including surfing and a different type of football, known as Australian Rules Football.

Surfing

Polynesians were known for their outstanding abilities in sea navigation, since they traveled around the ocean in small boats and canoes. They were also experts at surfing, a sport that existed there a long time before the Europeans arrived. It was most popular in Hawaii, where everyone enjoyed it, from warrior chiefs to farmers, women, children, and even grandparents.

Hawaii

Rugby

New Zealand's national rugby union team, nicknamed the All Blacks, are one of the top-ranking teams in the world.

Before each match they perform a traditional Maori dance, called the Haka. This dance includes chanting, grunting, and feet stamping. It was originally performed by warriors before going into battle.

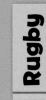

Australian Rules Football

Australian Rules Football is a contact sport that is believed to have begun in Melbourne in 1859.

Quick rule guide:

 played with an oval-shaped ball similar to a rugby ball

 two teams of 18 players each

 points scored by kicking the ball between two tall goal posts

 players may run and carry the ball the entire length of the field, provided they bounce or touch the ball on the ground at least once every 49 feet (15 m)

 the ball can be kicked or handballed (a handball is when the ball is held in one hand and punched with the fist of the other hand)

The All Blacks performing the Haka.

Rugby is also hugely popular among many of the Pacific island nations, with top teams from Tonga, Fiji, and Samoa.

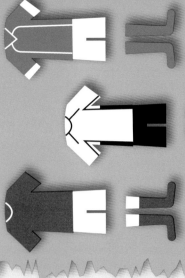

Samoa rugby kit

Fiji rugby kit

Tonga rugby kit

Bungee jumping

New Zealanders and thrill-seeking tourists have been bungee jumping there since the mid-1980s. The participant jumps off a high ledge, around 49 feet (15 m) high, with an elastic rope (bungee) attached to their ankles. When the bungee is fully stretched, the person springs back up.

Culture

Australia/Oceania has a rich multicultural society. Settlers from Europe, Asia, and the United States brought their traditions, beliefs, and culture with them. But the cultures of the Indigenous peoples are also an important part of the continent's heritage and continue to be celebrated today.

Nobel Prize winners

The Nobel Prize is an international award given to people who have made important advances in sciences (physics, chemistry, economics), medicine, literature, and peace, that have benefited humankind. Australia has produced 15 Nobel Prize winners, and New Zealand has produced 3 winners. Most of these winners worked in the fields of science or medicine.

Aboriginal culture

Australian Aboriginal culture is one of the longest-surviving cultures in the world. It lives on through ceremonies of dancing and singing, and the visual arts. Objects, such as the didgeridoo and the boomerang (below), have become internationally known symbols of their culture. The demand for artifacts and artwork provides Aboriginal communities with a source of income.

Aboriginal culture is strongly connected to the land. Artwork is often painted onto objects from the landscape, such as rocks and sheets of bark (above).

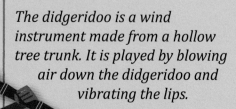

The didgeridoo is a wind instrument made from a hollow tree trunk. It is played by blowing air down the didgeridoo and vibrating the lips.

The boomerang is a wooden tool used in hunting. A boomerang is designed to return to the thrower.

Tattoos

The word "tattoo" comes from the Tahitian term tatau. In Tahiti and other Polynesian islands, tattooing is an important part of tribal culture. In the past, Samoan boys were tattooed as a sign that they had reached adulthood. In Fiji, it was more common to tattoo young women.

Patterns vary from island to island. Designs include images from nature, such as worms and starfish. Many of these designs are popular around the world today, and still remain important and symbolic for the descendants of the Indigenous Polynesians.

Samoa

Tahiti

Fiji

New Zealand film industry

New Zealand has become a top destination for making blockbuster movies. The country has a diverse landscape, offering scenery that suits fantasy films, such as the *Lord of the Rings* trilogy. It also has highly talented special effects companies, directors, and production teams.

New Zealand

Food and drink

Across Australia/Oceania, people enjoy a wide variety of local foods. There are foods from ancient Indigenous cultures, foods introduced during colonization, and foods brought over by more recent settlers. Chefs continue to develop this rich food tradition.

Noodles

Sago

Bush tucker

Bush tucker refers to food that can be sourced by someone living off the land. This ranges from the witchetty grubs, green ants, and snakes eaten by Indigenous Aboriginal people to the campsite foods of colonial settlers. These include:

Damper (bread baked in the ashes of a campfire, or in a camp oven or Dutch oven)

Bush oysters (lamb or bull testicles)

Pademelon or "paddymelon" (a small marsupial)

Meat pie

Anzac biscuits

Queensland

Pavlova

Barbecue

Yabby

Lamingtons

Lamingtons are a dessert from New Zealand named after Lord Lamington, the Governor of Queensland from 1896 to 1901. There are many stories telling how the cake came about. One story tells of the Lamingtons paying a visit to an ordinary household in the **outback**. In a panic to impress her important guests, the hostess quickly cut up a stale sponge cake and dipped it in chocolate and shredded coconut.

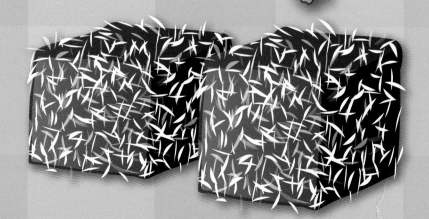

Pacific Rim cuisine

The different foods and methods of cooking from around the countries and islands of the Pacific Rim are often combined. This is known as Pacific Rim cuisine, where Asian spices and noodles are mixed with traditional produce from Hawaii or Guam. These foods are particularly popular in Australia and New Zealand. It reflects the effect immigration has had on creating a wider choice of foods on the menu.

Coconut shrimp with peanut sauce

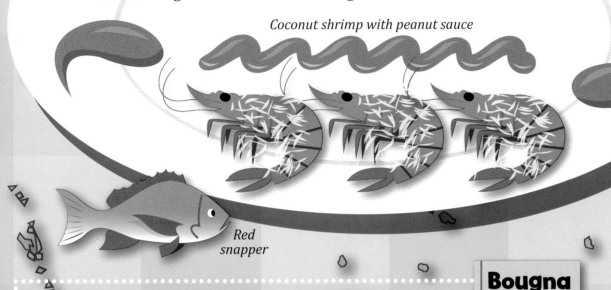

Red snapper

Taro

Breadfruit

Kiwi fruit

Roast lamb

Bougna

Bougna is a traditional dish from New Caledonia. It involves layers of food wrapped in a large bundle of banana leaves that are cooked in an underground oven for two hours. At the bottom are yams and taro, with bananas, plantains, or breadfruit placed over these, and fish or meat on top.

Wine

The warm climates of the **Southern Hemisphere** have helped to make Australia and New Zealand perfect places for growing grapevines and producing award-winning wines.

This woman is preparing her bougna dish.

Where is Antarctica?

Antarctica is the fifth-largest continent in the world, measuring 5,328,209 square miles (13,800,000 sq km). It sits at the very bottom of the Southern Hemisphere and is home to the South Pole. Its name Antarctica means "the opposite of Arctic."

Human inhabitants

Antarctica does not belong to any one country, although some countries have claimed parts of it as their own territory.

No one lives on Antarctica permanently, but approximately 5,000 scientists and support staff stay there for limited periods of time. They work in research stations that are maintained by various countries, including Japan, New Zealand, Argentina, United States, Russia, and the United Kingdom.

 = Research station

First human contact

No one is entirely sure who was the first person to set foot on Antarctica. Some think that it was an Anglo-American named Captain John Davis. He is thought to have arrived at Hughes Bay to hunt for seals.

Ross Ice Shelf

Ice shelves are floating sheets of ice that are connected to a landmass. The largest in Antarctica is the Ross Ice Shelf, which is roughly the size of France.

Mount Vinson is the highest mountain in Antarctica, measuring 16,049 feet (4,892 m) in height.

Australia

Antarctica

Giant cranch squid

Antarctic hair grass

Antarctic fur seal

Amundsen route
Scott route

South Pole

Sperm whale

Albatross

Hughes Bay

Emperor penguins

Elephant seal

28

Race to the South Pole

In December 1911, two expeditions set out to see who could reach the South Pole first. One was a Norwegian team led by Roald Amundsen. The other was a British team led by Captain Robert Falcon Scott.

They each took different routes, with Amundsen reaching the South Pole first on December 14, 1911. Scott's team finally arrived on January 25, 1912. Sadly, Scott's team never made it back to base camp. They all died in a blizzard on their return journey.

Polar desert

Antarctica has a polar desert landscape. It's too cold and windy for trees and shrubs to grow there, but there are low-growing lichens, grasses, and mosses. Seals and penguins survive well in this climate because they have thick fatty layers of skin that help keep them warm, and there is plenty of food to catch in the sea.

Ozone is a colorless gas that absorbs harmful ultraviolet rays that come from the Sun. The ozone layer protects Earth from these rays.

The hole in the ozone layer has caused ice shelves in Antarctica to melt, affecting its ecosystem. Until recent changes in pollution laws, the hole was getting larger, however it's now thought to be getting smaller.

The ozone hole

Earth can be displayed as a thermal map (shown right). It is showing us the amount of ozone in Earth's atmosphere over Antarctica. The purple area is where there is the least amount of ozone, referred to as the ozone hole.

Members of Roald Amundsen's expedition at the South Pole.

Further information

COUNTRY	POPULATION	SIZE SQ MI*	CAPITAL CITY	MAIN LANGUAGES
Australia	23, 795,663	2,988,885	Canberra	English
New Zealand	4,509,700	103,362.8	Wellington	English, Maori, NZ Sign Language
Polynesia:				
Samoa	194,492	1,093	Apia	Samoan, English
Tonga	106,478	288.4	Nuku'alofa	Tongan, English
Tuvalu	9,999	10	Funafuti	Tuvaluan, English
Melanesia:				
Papua New Guinea	7,821,000	178,702.5	Port Moresby	Hiri Motu, Tok Pisin, English
Fiji	905,949	7,055.6	Suva	English, Fijian, Fiji Hindi
Solomon Islands	609,883	11,156.7	Honiara	English, Melanesian pidgin
Vanuata	266,937	4,706.2	Port-Vila	Bislama, French, English
Micronesia:				
Federated States of Micronesia	105,681	271	Palikir	English (official)
Kiribati	104,488	313.1	South Tarawa	English, Gilbertese, I-Kiribati
Marshall Islands	70,983	69.9	Majuro	Marshallese, English
Palau	21,186	177.2	Ngerulmud, Melekeok State	English, Palauan
Nauru	9,488	8.1	Yaren (largest settlement)	Nauruan, English

*To arrive at square kilometers (sq km), divide a number in square miles (sq mi) by 0.386102.

Glossary

atoll
an island that is made of coral and shaped like a ring

climate
average weather conditions in a particular area

colonial
describing an area of land that is under political control and occupation of another country

convict
a person serving a prison sentence for having committed a criminal offence

drought
a prolonged period of low rainfall leading to a shortage of water

exports
goods or services sold to another country

imports
brings in goods from another country to sell

Indigenous
originating from, or naturally occurring in, a particular country or region

monolith
a very large single block of stone

monotremes
mammals that lay eggs instead of giving birth to live young, and the mothers feed their young with their milk

navigate
plan and direct the course of a ship or other forms of transportation by using instruments, such as a compass, and maps

ocean currents
seawater moving from one location to another, driven by wind, differences in water density, and rising and falling tides

outback
remote and usually uninhabited areas of land, such as the inland regions of Australia

sea level
the height of the sea's surface

southern hemisphere
section of Earth that is south of the equator

sovereign state
a country with territories overseas that it may not directly govern, but holds powers and influence that oversee how the territory is run

species
living things that have shared characteristics, such as human beings

tectonic plates
large slow-moving sections of Earth's surface

thermal geysers
springs of naturally hot water that intermittently send hot columns of water and steam into the air

tremors
a shaking movement that happens underground, usually before an earthquake

Index